THE YOM KIPPUR WAR

AARON ROSENBERG

THE ROSEN PUBLISHING GROUP, INC., NEW YORK

To all those who study war so that they can learn peace

Published in 2004 by The Rosen Publishing Group, Inc.
29 East 21st Street, New York, NY 10010

First Edition

Library of Congress Cataloging-in-Publication Data

Rosenberg, Aaron.
The Yom Kippur War/by Aaron Rosenberg.
    p. cm.—(War and conflict in the Middle East)
Summary: Examines the history behind the 1973 war between Israel and its Arab neighbors, Egypt and Syria backed by Iraq, Jordan, and Saudi Arabia, plus biographical notes on important figures and a look at the effects of this war.
Includes bibliographical references and index.
ISBN 0-8239-4553-7
1. Israel–Arab War, 1973—Juvenile literature. [1. Israel–Arab War, 1973. 2. Arab–Israeli conflict.]
I. Title. II. Series.
DS128.115.R678 2003
956.04'8—dc22
                                                    2003012460

Manufactured in the United States of America

CONTENTS

INTRODUCTION

Religion has stood at the center of many conflicts, and none more important than those in the Middle East. This part of the world is the birthplace of several of our oldest cultures and all three of the world's dominant religions: Judaism, Islam, and Christianity. Many Middle East locations are held sacred by two or even all three of these religions. Each feels they have the strongest right to those sacred places. This has led to wars over the centuries and has created strong hatred between the various sides. But while Christianity has its religious center in Rome, both Judaism and Islam focus upon the same ancient city: Jerusalem.

Jerusalem was once part of Palestine. When Israel was formed in 1948, Jerusalem was included in that territory, and Jews claimed the area as their homeland. This audacity angered the surrounding Arab nations, who felt they had an older right to the sacred city. They promptly attacked Israel, and this became only the first of many conflicts.

Over the next three decades, Israel and its neighbors continued to fight one another. Small skirmishes occurred almost every day, while larger battles and wars happened every few years. Even so, everyone was surprised when, in 1973, several Arab nations chose to attack Israel on Yom Kippur, the most important holiday in the Jewish religion. Israel was completely unprepared for such an attack. The war lasted only a few weeks, but it still stands as a turning point in Middle East politics. Its effects have lasted for decades and have affected everyone involved. It is known as the Yom Kippur War, though it has also been called the Ramadan War and the October War.

CHAPTER 1

SURPRISE ATTACK!

At 1:55 PM, Saturday, October 6, 1973, Jews were fasting and praying all throughout Israel. The highways were closed, as were the businesses and schools. This was a national holiday. Even the government had shut down. Prime Minister Golda Meir had closed a government meeting the night before by telling her advisers, "On Sunday we'll lay these problems before the cabinet."

The silence of that Saturday afternoon was shattered by the sound of artillery. Outside Tel Aviv, tanks appeared on the horizon. For months, Syria and Egypt had been massing their forces. The Israelis had seen these troop movements, of course, but thought little of it. Egypt's army seemed to be on training maneuvers. It had paraded about on its side of the Suez Canal. Syria looked like it was building up its defenses against the possibility of an Israeli attack.

Now that had changed.

The handful of Israeli soldiers still on duty found themselves facing hundreds of tanks in the Golan Heights on Israel's border with Syria. In the west along the Suez, thousands of Egyptian soldiers braced for battle. Israeli military leaders quickly issued orders, and men and women were called back from prayer and fasting. But the

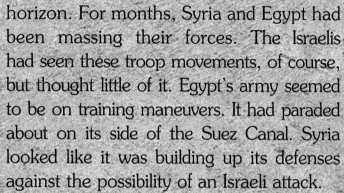

Orthodox Jews from Jerusalem perform the *kapparot* ceremony in preparation for Yom Kippur. This ritual represents the spiritual transformations that take place on Yom Kippur. Traditionally, a chicken is swung above one's head while a prayer is recited. Then, the chicken is slaughtered, and the entrails are fed to the birds.

Israeli army was in disarray—many of the troops had gone home for the holiday, and the defenses were barely manned. It was the perfect time for an attack and the last thing anyone in Israel, it seemed, had expected.

Intelligence Breakdown?

Some people in Israel had expected this attack. For weeks Israeli intelligence agents had received word that Egypt and Syria were going to attack. They didn't know exactly when, but they knew it was coming. It seemed, though, that the government had not believed the information. Why? Israel was overconfident. The last major conflict between Israel and its Arab neighbors was the Six-Day War in 1967. Israel had soundly defeated the combined Arab nations. It had claimed vast tracts of land from its opponents. Since then, only minor skirmishes had taken place. Israel had been able to hold its own against enemies on all sides. The Israeli leaders were convinced of their own nation's strength and of the weakness of their neighbors. They had determined these most recent reports were exaggerations and paranoia.

At 4 AM on Yom Kippur morning, Israel received word that Egypt and Syria would attack some time that afternoon. Again, the government chose not to act on this report. It did inform its ally, the United States, and had its military leaders start recalling soldiers to active duty. But the country's leaders decided to wait and see what happened before issuing a full-scale call to arms. If the threat turned out to be a false rumor, they didn't want to look foolish.

Yom Kippur

One of the worst things about the Yom Kippur War, for Israel, was that it occurred on the most important Jewish holiday. In the Jewish religion, the High Holidays are the two most important days of the year. One, Yom Kippur, is the day of atonement. This is the day when Jews traditionally pray for forgiveness for anything bad they have done during the previous year. According to the Bible, it was on this day that Abraham offered to sacrifice his only son, Isaac, to prove his love for God. God stopped the sacrifice just in time and told him to offer a ram instead. Then he said that every year Abraham and his sons should blow upon the shofar, or ram's horn, and that this would remind him of Abraham's devotion. In gratitude, God would then pardon them for anything they had done wrong that year.

Yom Kippur is a day entirely devoted to prayer and meditation. No work is allowed on that day, and it is a day of fasting as well.

The other High Holiday is Rosh Hashanah, the Jewish New Year.

Caught Off Guard

Instead, the threat proved very real, and the Israeli military sat unprepared. Only 177 tanks defended the Golan Heights. Supporting the tanks were just 50 artillery pieces (cannons, rocket launchers, mortars, and other weapons designed to fire upon tanks, planes, and other vehicles). Against these small defense forces, the Syrians amassed 1,400 tanks and more than 1,000 pieces of artillery! Along the Suez Canal, 500 Israeli soldiers found themselves facing more than 80,000 Egyptians!

Israel had built a 30-foot-high (9-meter-high) defensive border known as the Bar-Lev line just east of the Suez Canal. It was along this border that its troops were stationed. The Egyptians overran the Bar-Lev easily. Within a few hours, Egyptian forces controlled both sides of the canal. Israel had always assumed that, if Egypt ever attacked, the soldiers would take a long time crossing the Suez with their tanks and artillery. This would give Israeli soldiers time to prepare themselves more effectively. Instead, Egypt sent

Israeli tanks move from the Golan Heights to the Syrian border in 1973. While the Israeli government was vaguely aware of the Egyptian attack, Israeli forces were not.

its troops across with handheld Sagger antitank missiles and other light weapons. This strategy helped them reach the other side more quickly.

Egyptian infantry troops overran Israel's sand embankments and forced the defenders to retreat. Egyptian forces fired missiles to disable the few Israeli tanks on the scene. As troops gave protection from Israeli counterattack, more Egyptian forces were ferried across the canal. Now they brought along their tanks and artillery pieces. Egyptian troops were in place on Israeli soil within fifteen minutes of the first shot.

Egypt's Second Army took the northern portion of the canal. The Third Army claimed the southern portion. Using surface-to-air missiles, they shot down Israeli planes. This was a stunning defeat. Israel had grown accustomed to dominating the air in the Middle East. Now it found its air force unable to control the skies. Egypt claimed the entire east bank of the Suez Canal and lost only 208 soldiers in the attack.

Fighting on the Golan Heights was less one-sided and, thus, not as decisive. By the end of the day, however, Syrian forces had taken control of the lands directly across Syria's border with the Golan Heights. They then began an advance toward the Sea of Galilee. If this continued, they would easily reclaim the southern half of the Golan as well. Once entrenched, the Syrians could hold off Israeli forces much more easily.

Interestingly, it was not hard for Israel to mobilize its reserves. Everyone was either at home or in synagogue, and so the soldiers were easy to find. Getting everyone moving again and organizing a plan of defense, however, was difficult. Egypt and Syria had momentum. Israel was stumbling and trying to regroup. Its defensive lines had already been breached, or run over. The military had to figure out new places to stand and fight. Worse, each delay meant more territory lost and made it harder to push the Arab armies back. Israel had already taken a worse beating and had lost more land than in all its previous wars combined.

The Golan Heights is an area of land northeast of Israel that is bordered by Jordan, Syria, and Lebanon. Israel gained control of the area during the Six-Day War. Here, Israeli forces defend the area against the Syrian army. Today, the Golan Heights is still under Israeli control.

Empty Reassurances

On October 6 at 6:30 PM, Golda Meir addressed Israel. She told her people about the war and the government's plans. She claimed that the Israeli military was "beating back the assault" and said that "[t]he enemy has suffered grave losses." She also mentioned that Israeli intelligence had anticipated the attack and that "[w]e were not caught by surprise." She urged the people not to panic and reassured them that everything was under control. She also reminded them that Israel had not started this conflict and that the government had asked other countries to intervene in the hopes of preventing the war. The last two statements, at least, were true—Israel had not begun this war, and Meir had informed America of the planned attack and asked it for help.

The Battle of Latakia

On October 7, the second day of the war, an interesting battle occurred. It was not considered very important at the time. First, it was a naval battle, and Israel had never been known for having a powerful navy. The nation was respected and feared for its air force, but its navy had always been considered something of a joke. Second, the battle did not take place in Israeli waters or even in the contested territories.

Syria had a reasonably strong navy, including several missile boats. These were considered the greatest danger to opposing forces. They could be used against planes or even

Golda Meir: Prime Minister of Israel (1969–1974)

Golda Meir in 1969

Golda Meir was born in Kiev, Russia, in 1898. Her family immigrated to the United States in 1906, settling in Milwaukee, Wisconsin. In 1915, she joined the Zionist group Poalei Zion ("Workers of Zion"), and in 1921, she and her husband Morris Meyerson moved to a kibbutz (communal farm) in Palestine. In 1946, Meir became head of the Jewish Agency's political department. The Jewish Agency helped Jews worldwide to immigrate to the homeland. During World War II, the agency helped to rescue Jews from Nazi persecution and murder. She went on to become the executive of the Jewish Agency and helped raise funds in America to support Israel's War of Independence (1948). In 1948, Prime Minister David Ben-Gurion appointed Meir a member of the provisional government. She became foreign minister in 1956; ten years later she became secretary-general of the Mapai Party and then secretary-general of the new Labor Party. When Prime Minister Levi Eshkol passed away in early 1969, Meir was chosen to replace him.

Meir negotiated an unprecedented level of both financial and military aid for Israel, including weapons and support from the United States. She did her best to calm the citizens during the Yom Kippur War but felt personally responsible for the nation's failure to anticipate and prepare for the attack. After all, Meir had been warned by King Hussein of Jordan several days before, but she had let her advisers convince her that the threat was not real. In June 1974, Meir resigned from both her office and politics, although in November 1977, she was present at the Knesset (Israeli legislature) to greet Egyptian president Anwar Sadat on his first official visit to Israel.

land-based targets (such as buildings) as easily as against other ships. The missile boats were harbored in the port of Latakia, along the Syrian coast. There they awaited orders. The Israeli navy was sent out to lure the Syrians out of Latakia, fight them, and destroy them. This would have been a simple matter for a powerful navy. Unfortunately, the Israelis did not have many vessels. They were also using a new antiship missile, the Gabriel, which had never been tested in combat. The Gabriel had half the range of the Syrians' Soviet-made missiles. Defense against such missiles took the form of electronic jamming devices. Missiles found their targets using radar, which locked onto a target found using electronic mapping. Jamming devices scrambled the mapping capabilities of targeting radar. These electronic jamming devices had never been used in combat before, either.

An Israeli task force of five ships moved toward Latakia. It met only a single Syrian torpedo boat along the way and sank it easily. A second ship, a large and clumsy minesweeper, was spotted next. It, too, was sunk. Then three of the Syrian missile boats appeared. The Israelis used jamming systems to confuse the Syrians' Styx missiles and fired chaff (airborne debris) designed to set the missiles off prematurely (the missiles would hit the chaff instead of the Israeli ships and would blow up while still a safe distance away). The countermeasures worked perfectly, and all three Syrian ships were destroyed. Israel's naval ships quickly sealed off the port of Latakia from the rest of the Syrian navy.

Moshe Dayan: Defense Minister of Israel (1967–1974)

Moshe Dayan in 1973

Dayan was born on a kibbutz near Lake Kinneret in Israel on May 20, 1915. At fourteen he joined the Haganah, an underground organization that protected Jewish settlements from Arab attacks. In 1939, Dayan was arrested and imprisoned. Upon his release in 1941, he joined the British army. He lost his right eye during a battle in Lebanon. In 1948, Dayan became commander of the Israeli forces along the Jerusalem front. In 1953, he became chief of staff of the armed forces, and three years later he led the Suez campaign. He was elected to the Knesset in 1959 and was minister of agriculture for five years. Levi Eshkol appointed Dayan as minister of defense shortly before the Six-Day War in 1967. Dayan not only made the crucial attack plan in that war, but he also organized the cease-fire a few days later. He retained his post when Golda Meir became prime minister.

Dayan firmly believed that Egypt and Syria lacked the power and the conviction to attack Israel again so soon after the Six-Day War. He believed in keeping the Israeli forces ready, but he also believed that they would not face an attack for several more years. Dayan also fell for Anwar Sadat's deceit and believed that the Egyptian forces massing along the Suez were merely on training missions. Dayan took most of the blame for the lack of preparation, casualties, and damages the nation had received during the war. The public demanded his resignation. He agreed to step down in 1974. Dayan returned to politics a few years later as minister of foreign affairs. Later, he even served as Israel's negotiator during the peace talks with Egypt. However, many Israelis continued to look upon him as a failure who had cost the country many lives.

This battle was one of the first Israeli victories of the war. It also proved an important battle for military techniques. Before this, no one had ever used electronic countermeasures against missiles. The Israelis proved that this could work. They also demonstrated that small, fast ships could take out larger and more powerful vessels. The Israeli navy had never been considered a real threat until that day.

Early Retreat

Having already lost their fortifications, the Israeli forces had no choice but to retreat. Defense Minister Moshe Dayan ordered the army to pull back to higher ground in the Golan Heights. To do this, the army passed through the mountains of Jebel Maara and Jebel Yalek. Dayan's generals were not happy to retreat within their own borders, but they quickly followed orders. One commander, a reserve major general named Ariel Sharon, requested permission to counterattack. He was located along the Sinai Peninsula front and wanted to take his troops across the Suez Canal, cutting between the Second and Third Armies of the Egyptians and attacking them from behind. Dayan denied his request.

CHAPTER 2

A LOOK BACK

Wars don't occur in a vacuum—something has to happen to cause them. So what started the Yom Kippur War? Actually, the Middle East had been filled with tension and fighting for more than twenty-five years. The nations there had already gone to war against one another several times. The Yom Kippur War was simply the latest in a long string of conflicts.

Israel v. the Arab Nations

Ever since Israel's creation in 1948, its Arab neighbors have attacked it. In part, this was political. Moreover, the new Jewish nation had been foisted upon them by the United Nations. The Arab nations saw this as a Jewish land grab, taking away land from existing Palestine. Several of the Arab nations had considered the Palestinians already living on that land as allies.

Conflicts also arose because of religious hatred. Israel was intended as a Jewish homeland, and the Jews claimed that the land belonged to them from biblical times. They used passages from the Bible to prove their argument. The Palestinians disagreed. They had been living on those lands for centuries already. They felt the

For Jews, the promise of their own nation lifted their spirits after the atrocities that befell them during World War II. A boat crowded with hopeful Jewish refugees pulls into port at Haifa in 1946.

Jews were intruders. The surrounding Arab nations agreed with the Palestinians.

The Jews also made good scapegoats for neighboring Arab governments. Problems at home threatened Arab leaders throughout the region. Unemployment was high. Food shortages threatened lives. Arab rule in the region was brutal. By blaming the Jews for lack of trade and other ills, Arab leaders focused the people's anger upon the new nation.

Arabs fight Jews from behind the walls of the Holy City, Jerusalem, on March 5, 1948. Because the area is religiously significant to both Islam and Judaism, it is a source of massive conflict.

It did not help matters that Israel proved more than capable at defending itself. The first war was fought against Israel's independence. It began the same day the new nation was created. A combined Arab attack failed, and Israel claimed more land as a result. Later battles went much the same way—though vastly outnumbered each time, Israel won most of the conflicts and gained territory with each war.

The worst of these, from an Arab standpoint, was the Six-Day War. The Israeli army captured the Sinai Peninsula, the Golan Heights, the Gaza Strip, and the West Bank of the Jordan River. With each victory came another insult to its Arab neighbors. The Arabs in turn found another reason to unite against this upstart nation.

Many of the Arab nations had disputes with Israel, but none more than Egypt and Syria. These two nations had been at the forefront of each attack on the Jewish state. As its immediate neighbors to the west and north, they had also been the ones to lose the most territory. No one was surprised that either country would want to attack Israel again. The only shock was that they had planned their attack so carefully and so cleverly. Arab nations attacking Israel had never before so closely coordinated attacks.

A Change in Egypt

Egyptian ruler Gamal Abdel Nasser died in 1970. Nasser had been Egypt's president since 1954. He was a leader in the nation's independence from British control back in 1953. He had also been one of Israel's strongest opponents.

Nasser's successor, Anwar Sadat, was considered more businesslike than the militaristic Nasser.

However, Sadat had several problems to solve. The first was Egypt's humiliating defeat in the Six-Day War. The country had lost valuable land in the Sinai. Egyptians still demanded revenge against Israel. The second problem was Egypt's military strength. Again, the Six-Day War had destroyed most of Egypt's military hardware. Nasser had been forced to rely more and more upon aid from the Communist Soviet Union. Sadat knew that the Soviets would try to pressure him, too, to rule Egypt more as they ruled their own country. Sadat disliked letting anyone else control Egypt. He knew that he would need to demonstrate the nation's strength quickly. The obvious solution was to attack, and defeat, Israel. But how? Nasser had been passionate and charismatic, but Sadat was careful. He understood that simply launching another attack wouldn't work. He had to find a way to take Israel by surprise.

Other Nations

Sadat knew that he couldn't defeat Israel on his own. He needed allies. He appealed to the other Arab nations for support and alliance. Some of them refused. Jordan, for one, did not want another war. Saudi Arabia and Iraq both declined to participate in an all-out attack. Both nations helped fund the attack, though, and provided some troops. Only one nation was happy to participate: Syria.

Syria was Israel's northern neighbor. It had lost a great deal of land in the Six-Day War, just as Egypt had. Syria also

Anwar Sadat: President of Egypt (1970–1981)

Anwar Sadat was born in Egypt in 1918 to poor Egyptian Sudanese parents. He entered the Royal Military Academy in 1936, and there met Gamal Abdel Nasser. The two cadets became close friends. Even though they had very different personalities, they formed the Free Officers Movement together. The Free Officers were determined to overthrow Egypt's king and release the country from British control. Sadat was one of the nine men who led the 1952 revolution and transformed Egypt from a monarchy to a Socialist regime. When Nasser died of a sudden heart attack in 1970, Sadat succeeded him as president of Egypt.

Egyptian president Anwar Sadat

In 1977, Sadat surprised everyone by visiting Israel. Two years later, the two nations signed the Camp David Peace Accords. As a result, Israel returned land to Egypt (and agreed to help establish a Palestinian state) in exchange for a promise of peace. Sadat and Menachem Begin, Israel's prime minister, were awarded the Nobel Peace Prize in 1978 for their efforts. On October 6, 1981, while reviewing a military parade in Cairo, Sadat was shot and killed by a trio of fundamentalist soldiers who saw him as a traitor.

had a history of alliance with Egypt. At one point, the two countries had merged into the United Arab Republic (1958–1961). More recently, the radical Baath Party had pulled off a coup (government overthrow) and taken control of Syria. A new legislature had been formed. The former minister of defense, Hafiz al-Assad, was elected president. Assad was eager to prove his control of Syria. He also wanted to show the world that Syria was now a major power. Finally, Assad wanted to renew his nation's ties to Egypt, especially since both countries received a good deal of aid from the Soviet Union. Just days after his election as president, Assad had talked with Egypt about joining a new coalition. All of this proved useful to Sadat's plans. Assad enthusiastically agreed to participate in a new attack on their mutual enemy.

The Superpowers

Although three Middle East nations were fighting the Yom Kippur War, a second conflict was taking place between the world's top two superpowers. The United States and the Soviet Union had been competing for Middle East influence for years. Both had achieved mixed results. Israel was strongly allied with the United States. Iraq and Egypt had trade and military relations with the Soviet Union. Both superpowers helped arm and train their allies.

In 1969, the Soviets sent a squadron of MiG-21 fighters to Egypt—complete with pilots and ground crews! The MiGs helped defend Egyptian air space during the War of Attrition,

Hafiz al-Assad: President of Syria (1971–2000)

Hafiz al-Assad was born on October 6, 1930, in the mountains of Syria. He was schooled under the Alawite sect of Sunni Islam. At fourteen, Assad was sent to a French school in the town of Latakia. At sixteen, he joined the nationalist Baath Party. Assad graduated from the Syrian Military Academy in 1955 as an air force lieutenant. He was one of the five men who led the March 8 revolution in 1963. His reward was appointment as general secretary of the Baath Party and commander of the air force. Assad became prime minister

Syrian president Hafiz al-Assad in 1987

and minister of defense in 1970. On March 12, 1971, the Syrian Arab Republic held its first referendum, and Assad was elected president. By late August of that year, he had been promoted to secretary-general of the Baath Party.

Assad hated that Syria was seen by most nations as weak and, at best, a minor military threat. He wanted the world to respect him and fear him. He also wanted to reclaim all the Golan Heights territory that Israel had taken in the Six-Day War. Assad had a personal stake in all this, as well. He had been Syria's defense minister during the Six-Day War and had taken his nation's defeat personally. Striking back at Israel gave Assad the chance to avenge his wounded pride. Unfortunately for him, Assad overestimated his nation's military strength and Anwar Sadat's willingness to assist Syria in battle.

an ongoing conflict between Egypt and Israel following the Six-Day War. The Israelis turned to the United States for support. They too purchased arms for the ongoing War of Attrition.

On August 7, 1970, the Rogers Plan went into effect. It called for a cease-fire to the killing happening across the various enemy borders. The Egyptians pushed against this truce the very next day by moving their Soviet-supplied antiaircraft batteries near the banks of the Suez Canal.

During a cease-fire with Egypt in 1970, an Israeli soldier surveys the Suez Canal. The Suez Canal links the Mediterranean and Red Seas and was considered international property until Egypt declared ownership in 1956.

Israel did not respond, perhaps to show that it was willing to abide by the Rogers Plan. It did complain to the U.S. leadership in Washington, D.C. The U.S. State Department claimed there was no proof that the Egyptians had moved the antiaircraft batteries. A few days later, Israel produced aerial photographs proving its case. The United States did not insist that the Soviet weapons be removed, however. Such a move could be taken as direct intervention into the ongoing conflict between Arab nations and Israel. Instead, the United States chose to supply Israel with additional weapons.

If the United States had stepped in and insisted that the Soviet Union remove its weapons from the Suez Canal, the Yom Kippur War might have gone differently. Those antiaircraft guns took a heavy toll on Israel at the start of the battle. On the other hand, if the superpowers had been fully involved, Russia might have sent more troops to help Egypt, and the war might have grown even larger and taken a heavier toll.

Misdirection

Sadat was very clever with his preparations for the Yom Kippur attack. He knew that Aman (Israeli military intelligence) was watching Egypt closely. If the Israeli Defense Force (IDF) knew he was going to attack, it would be ready for him.

Part of Sadat's strategy was to become the boy who cried wolf. In 1971, Sadat announced that Egypt would attack Israel. He called that year the year of decision. But the year ended without an attack. The next year, he continued to threaten war, but took no real military action. By 1973, Aman was convinced that Sadat was only bluffing.

The second part of Sadat's strategy was concealment. Only a handful of people knew the full battle plans: Sadat and his minister of war, Ahmed Ismail Ali, in Egypt, and no more than ten people in Syria. The Egyptian general staff were told about the war on October 1, just days before the attack. Field commanders received their orders on October 5. The rest of the military did not find out about the war until a few hours before the October 6 assault. This secrecy kept Aman from finding out until it was too late that Sadat was serious this time.

The third part of Sadat's strategy was to provide false clues. He allowed military schools to reopen and soldiers to take personal time. Those troops arranged along the Suez Canal were instructed to walk about out of uniform and to play games. To all appearances, the Egyptian military had no intention of fighting anyone and certainly not anytime soon.

Preliminary Moves

In August 1973, the Syrians moved troops and weapons along the Golan front. The troops brought along a network of surface-to-air missiles. Once set up, the network covered not only the skies over Golan but also the air space over the Syrian troops. Israel noticed this activity but did not take it any more seriously than Egypt's previous bluffs.

A Matter of Timing

Egypt and Syria worked together on the battle plans for the attack, which they called Operation Badr. One of the last things they decided was the date. In mid-September they still had not chosen when to launch their first attacks. Once the day had been selected, the next question was the time. The two nations disagreed on that. The Syrians wanted to attack at dawn, with the sun behind them—it might make the Israeli soldiers blink and wince in the glare, which would make them less effective. The Egyptians, however, preferred sunset. By then, the day would be almost over, and no one would expect an attack that close to nightfall. Neither country would agree to the other's proposal. Finally, on October 3, the two reached a compromise. They would attack at 2 PM. The sun would still be high enough to cause a glare, but it would be late enough that no one would expect anything.

Also, Israel knew that Syria would never attack it without aid from Egypt. Since Israel was still convinced that Egypt wasn't planning an attack, it never understood the Syrian movements until it was too late.

One other event led the Israeli military into a false sense of security. On September 13, 1973, the Israeli Air Force (IAF) shot down twelve Syrian jets during a reconnaissance mission over Syrian territory. The IAF lost only one jet. This reinforced Israel's belief that the Arabs would never risk an attack against it.

Despite this, Israel did send more infantry and tanks to the Golan Heights at the end of September. The increasing

Anxious not to waste any more time in defending the Golan Heights, Israeli tanks move up the Golan Heights following an attack launched across the Suez Canal by Syria and Egypt. The Israelis were fighting a two-front war and had to carefully position their troops where they were most effective.

number of Syrian troops there had prompted the move, but Israel did it more to show it was not frightened than because it genuinely expected conflict.

On October 4, Soviet advisers and their families left Egypt and Syria. To many of the Israeli leaders, this was the first sign of real danger. The fact that families were leaving told them that something big was going to happen, and soon. However, Sadat had expelled several thousand Soviet advisers from Egypt after the Soviet Union refused to give him more weapons. So more people leaving was seen as nothing to worry over.

The following day, aerial photographs showed that Egyptian and Syrian forces along the borders had increased. Members of Israeli intelligence and officers in the military suspected that the Arab forces might attack. But they were not sure, and their superiors still claimed it would never happen. So now the Jewish nation turned its attention to the High Holidays and the observance of Yom Kippur.

CHAPTER 3

ARAB CONQUEST

From the very start, the attacks went exactly as Sadat and Assad had planned. Israel was taken completely by surprise, and its soldiers were unprepared. In fact, most of them weren't even on the battlefield! After four days, the Arab armies seemed totally in control. The two Arab leaders were delighted. They stood to regain not only their lost land but also their tattered pride.

Israeli Losses

By October 8, the Syrian forces were only a few miles from the eastern shore of Lake Tiberias and the Jordan River. Helicopters dropped commandos on Mount Hermon, and they rapidly claimed that strategic location. Other troops attacked the city of Migdal-Ha'Emek and inflicted heavy casualties.

Israeli leaders were worried about the Syrian advance because the tanks and artillery were passing so close to towns and villages. They feared massive damage and human casualties. Dayan ordered the military to deploy nuclear missiles in case the Syrians crossed the original boundaries set by the United Nations. He ordered that the nuclear weapons were only to be used as a last resort. Israel's air force had already been weakened

Israeli soldiers carry a wounded comrade to safety amidst the fighting between Israel and Egypt and Syria. During the Yom Kippur War, approximately 2,500 Israeli soldiers died in combat.

by Syrian missile strikes at its northern air bases. Many crippled planes lay on the ground, but some pilots managed to get their fighters aloft. Pilots tried to take out the Syrian missile placements in the Golan Heights. This plan would limit the Syrians' ability to counter aerial attacks. The attempt failed to completely neutralize the Syrian missiles. The Israeli pilots did knock out one battery of missiles but lost six jets in the process.

While Israel focused its attention on Syria, Egypt took the time to dig in where its army had taken land on both sides of the Suez Canal. Israel launched its first counterattack against Egypt on October 8. Reserve major general Avraham Adan, whose troops were placed along the northern portion of the canal, attacked in concert with Sharon's forces along the center. Unfortunately, Adan ran into the Second Army's main forces and took heavy losses. He withdrew to the east, and Sharon's troops, who had been sent south, were instead told to go north to cover the region Adan had just left. The attack was in complete shambles, in part from faulty communications. Suddenly, Israel's defense along the canal looked weaker than ever.

Air Raid

On October 9, the Israeli government decided to attack strategic and economic centers in Syria. It hoped this would upset the Syrians and make them lose focus. With luck, they might even pull back their forces to defend their own homes. The first targets were the Syrian General Command and the Syrian Air Force Command buildings (the two sat side by side) in Damascus.

The Israeli Air Force sent sixteen Phantom jets on the mission. Pilots were told to fly at low altitude and radio silence. One of the jets had mechanical problems and returned to base, but the others proceeded. Heavy clouds covered Syria at first, but by the time the jets reached Damascus the clouds had dispersed. The first group of jets dropped their bombs and wheeled about to head home. Syrian antiaircraft batteries hit two of the jets. One jet was

An Israeli Skyhawk flies over an infantry division during the battle for Golan Heights. The Israeli Defense Force was formed shortly after the founding of Israel in 1948. One of its strongest branches is the air force.

destroyed, the pilot killed, and the navigator captured. The other jet was damaged but successfully returned to base.

The second Phantom group never reached Damascus. The clouds had returned, and the Syrians were now ready for a second attack. Nonetheless, the buildings had been badly damaged, and the Syrian commanders were forced to move to new locations. This victory demonstrated that the IAF could bypass Syria's main defense force at any time. It gave the Israelis hope, as it filled the Syrians with fear and doubt.

The Golan Heights lies war-torn on October 9, 1973, during the Yom Kippur War. Israeli troops *(right)* advance through the smoking rubble, while a Syrian tank *(left)* lies overturned in a ditch.

A Second Attempt

Ariel Sharon had wanted to counterattack the Egyptians from the second day of the war, but he had been denied. Then Sharon and Adan's counterattack had fallen apart. So the next day, Sharon launched his own counterattack from the south, despite orders to hold his position. His men moved through the area called the Chinese Farm, a gap between the Second and Third Armies. Adan used the time to regroup his own forces and form a stronger defense against the Egyptian advance. Although Sharon's attack did help slow Egyptian troops, he had acted against orders, and his superior, Lieutenant General Haim Bar-Lev (who had been given temporary control of the southern command that same day), requested Sharon's dismissal.

Meanwhile, the first Israeli reserve forces had finally mobilized and moved into position in the north and the south. Colonel Ori Orr and Major General Moshe Peled commanded the southern sector and moved their tanks and men to block the Syrian advance. On the Syrian side, General Tewtik Jehani, who was in charge of the southern sector, saw that his north side would be vulnerable and chose to pull back slightly rather than letting himself be cut off. This allowed Orr and Peled to regain territory to the south and to position their own men more effectively.

Conflicting Orders

Egypt had problems of its own. On October 10, the First Egyptian Mechanized Brigade advanced south toward Ras

Help from Neighboring Arab States

Egypt and Syria were the two nations openly attacking Israel, but they were not the only Arab countries involved. Iraq sent a squadron of Hunter jets to Egypt. It also provided more than 18,000 soldiers and several hundred tanks in the Golan Heights. Its MiG fighter jets also took part in the attack on the Golan. Saudi Arabia sent a brigade of 3,000 men to Syria. Their main use was to block any Israeli forces advancing on Damascus. Libya sent Mirage fighters. Algeria sent squadrons of fighter jets and bombers, and it also sent dozens of tanks and several armored brigades. Tunisia sent more than 1,000 soldiers to work with Egyptian troops. Sudan sent 3,500 men. Morocco sent hundreds of troops, too. Lebanon provided Syria with radar units and allowed Palestinians to shell Israeli settlements from its lands. Even Jordan sent two armored brigades and three artillery batteries to aid Syria.

Other Arab nations helped with money and equipment. Libya gave Egypt $1 billion to help pay for military equipment. Saudi Arabia and Kuwait paid for most of the other costs, which are estimated at around $3 billion.

Sudar. This move put it beyond the range of the protective missile umbrella, which was set up to fire SAM (surface-to-air missiles) at approaching planes. Israeli major general Yeshayahu Gavish noticed the movement and ordered an air strike. The strike destroyed the Egyptian brigade. This put the Egyptians in a dilemma.

Egypt's chief of staff, Saad el-Shazli, insisted that his troops could not move any faster than the missile umbrella could be relocated. Therefore, his troops could not race to cover the rest of the Sinai. On the other hand, Minister of War Ahmed Ismail Ali insisted that the only way to defend against such attack was to sweep down over the Sinai and take control of it quickly. What happened instead was that Israeli forces were able to regain control over much of the Sinai because Jehani had decided to consolidate his position instead of attacking.

On the other side, Israel was considering whether it should attempt to cross the canal. Doing so would give it a strong position against the Egyptian forces. The problem was that Egypt now had 1,000 tanks on the east side of the canal. If Israeli forces were sent to the west side of the canal, there might not be enough troops and equipment to block an Egyptian advance across the Sinai. The general staff decided to wait and focus on defending its own land before it went after Egypt directly. This proved to be a wise choice. Part of the problem for the Arab forces had always been that they were ultimately several different armies. Each army had its own objectives and its own areas to defend. There was no central command that directed all the forces at one time or to a single target.

Israel had to worry about enemies on all sides, but for defense it could fall back and block from each direction, taking that time to form a new strategy. If Egypt and Syria had been better coordinated with one another, they could have kept pressure on Israel from both sides. Instead, Israel was able to focus on Syria first and then deal with Egypt after the Syrian threat had been largely eliminated.

CHAPTER 4

ISRAEL RECOUPS

By October 11, enough Israeli troops had reached the Golan Heights to properly oppose Syria. They soon drove the Syrians back beyond the 1967 armistice line, then began marching into Syria itself. In one particularly impressive battle, Israeli tanks annihilated the Syrians facing the Seventh Brigade. By dawn, only seven Israeli tanks were left, but more than 500 Syrian tanks had been destroyed in the valley below them!

Israeli leaders knew better than to become invaders. They were only concerned with forcing Syria to retreat and teaching it not to attack them again. Besides, if Israeli troops advanced too far into Syria, the Soviets might step in to block them. Israel was not large enough or strong enough to oppose the Soviet Union directly. So Israeli units reached a town halfway between Kunaitra (the main city in the Golan Heights) and Damascus. Then they stopped. That was far enough to prove their point. When they felt that the Syrians were safely out of their lands, the Israelis turned their attention back to the Egyptians.

Fatal Hesitation

The Israeli general staff was worried about the Egyptian forces massed along the east

Israeli troops, waiting for the next plan of attack, scatter themselves across a stretch of desert on October 23, 1973. The Israelis had to act quickly to secure their lands from the Syrians and Egyptians.

bank of the Suez. This was on the Israeli side of the Bar-Lev line. A counterattack had been planned, but they decided to hold off on that. Instead, on October 12, orders were given to take defensive positions. Once the Egyptian attack had been fended off, then Israel could launch its own offensive.

But Sadat hesitated. He knew that committing all of his forces to this attack was risky. It would also carry him past his objective. He had already gained both sides of the Suez, which had been his major goal. Still, he and Assad were allies, and Assad demanded support for his beaten troops. On October 13, Sadat finally responded and launched an attack into Sinai to distract the Israelis. He had waited too long, though. Now the Israeli forces were better prepared. Sharon's forces heavily defended the central sector.

The following day, the Egyptian attack began in earnest. Egypt's objective was to take the Mitla and Gidi Passes, two critical spots in the Sinai. If it could hold those two positions, the Israelis would be forced to approach them along narrow paths. Then Egypt would hold the advantage. This was the largest tank-to-tank battle ever fought between the two countries. Almost from the start, Israeli forces held the upper hand. By the end of the day, they had lost ten tanks, but Egypt had lost nearly 300. Even with its superior numbers, this was a serious blow to Egypt. Part of the problem was that every time Egyptian forces moved out from under their missile umbrella, Israeli fighter jets cut them down. Egyptian chief of staff Shazli demanded that they move back to the west bank of the Suez and take

Ecstatic Egyptian soldiers boost morale by holding up a picture of their president, Anwar Sadat, in October 1973. Egyptians still felt embarrassed over the outcome of the Six-Day War, but their efforts during the Yom Kippur War gave them a renewed sense of national pride.

up defensive positions, but both Sadat and his minister of war refused to retreat and continued the attack. They should have listened. By the following night, Sharon's forces had pushed through the Chinese Farm and were approaching the canal along the northern coast of the Great Bitter Lake. They had cut between the Second and Third Armies and were looking at crossing the canal almost unopposed.

Additional Support

Along the Syrian front, Assad grew desperate. Israeli troops were halfway to Damascus and had begun shelling the outskirts of the city. Sadat's men were occupied in the Sinai and could not offer any aid. So Assad turned to Iraq and Jordan for help.

Iraq agreed to help and sent an Iraqi division into the southern sector, near Tel al Mal and Tel Maschara. The division attacked the Israelis three times but did not bother to coordinate properly with the Syrians. The Iraqi troops were too isolated and were easily defeated each time. A second division tried to cross eastern Syria to join the war, but the Israeli Air Force struck first and severely damaged the division, making it completely useless. Now Iraqi soldiers littered the battlefield as well. Syria was in no better shape than before.

Crossing the Canal

Sharon's forces crossed the canal early on October 16 and struck the Egyptians from the rear. The attack shattered the

Egyptian ranks. At the same time, more tanks and troops attacked from the front, cutting right through the Egyptian forces. Additional Israeli soldiers moved into the Chinese Farm corridor to widen their hold on that location. This move was to make sure they would have enough room to send most of their force across the canal safely. Shazli demanded again that the Egyptian troops be withdrawn to the canal's west bank, but Minister of War Ali refused.

The Israelis were also bickering. Sharon had established a beachhead on the western bank of the Suez and was expanding his hold there. But the general staff still felt the Chinese Farm was too thinly defended. It wanted more forces there to widen the corridor. Sharon refused to listen and concentrated on finding and attacking SAM batteries instead. This move let Israeli planes attack more easily and safely, but it was against direct orders from Sharon's superiors. On October 17, Adan's forces also crossed the canal, but they were supposed to cross the day before—Adan had been forced to delay while his men widened the corridor, as Sharon had been ordered to do. Bar-Lev, infuriated at Sharon's continued disobedience, again requested his removal. But Sharon was getting results, and Bar-Lev's request was denied a second time.

CHAPTER 5

A GRADUAL STOP

wo weeks after the war began, Arab forces were in trouble. It had taken Israel longer to rally than Egypt and Syria had expected. Once it had, however, the Israeli troops proved to be extremely effective. The Arab force, on the other hand, had divided into Egyptian and Syrian armies. Their lack of unity had weakened them severely. It was time for Israel to finish the job.

Home Defense

Assad's forces had been pushed back into Syria, and by October 20 Israelis had recaptured the peaks on Mount Hermon. Two days later they held the entire mountain, although they lost several soldiers in the process. Israel now dominated the Syrian-Israeli border, and its troops were not far from Damascus. Close-range shelling had begun there, and Assad was terrified. Not only had he failed to reclaim the Golan Heights, but now his capital city was under attack by enemy forces camped just outside. If no one stepped in, the entire nation could easily be lost!

Egypt was not faring much better. An Israeli base had been established on the western bank of the Suez, and from there it directed its attacks against Egypt.

Israeli troops successfully pushed the Syrians out of the Golan Heights. The Israelis avoided pushing too far into Syria for fear of launching a larger conflict with the Soviet Union, which supported Syria.

By October 21, Adan's forces had taken the territory near Suez City. Sadat had sent the Third Army to counter this attack, but the army ended up being encircled. Now it was in danger of being completely destroyed. Sharon's forces had gone north and west, taking Ismailiya. The Second Army was now in danger of being cut off from support and supplies. Sharon's forces continued to advance and had taken up positions less than 43 miles (70 kilometers) from Cairo itself.

The Superpowers Collide

The Soviet Union was horrified. Its allies were in grave danger. If Egypt and Syria were destroyed, the Soviets would lose their influence in the Middle East. The Soviet Union threatened to intervene with its own troops. This would bring the United States in on the other side. Many feared the start of World War III. No one wanted that, certainly not the superpowers.

At the same time, Egypt and Syria both faced military defeat. The Soviets invited United States secretary of state Henry Kissinger to Moscow. Kissinger flew to Moscow to work with Communist Party chairman Leonid Brezhnev. They agreed that it would be best if the fighting ended. They then focused on writing a jointly acceptable United Nations Security Council resolution.

Sadat was happy to agree. He had actually accomplished his major goal. He had demonstrated that Egypt was strong enough to pose a threat and that the lands Israel captured should be returned. Now he just wanted Israeli troops back on their side of the Suez and his own cities safe from harm.

Assad was less happy. He had wanted to recapture lost territory, too. Instead, he had been pushed back into his own capital. While he recognized the need to stop fighting, his pride had been badly wounded. He was too angry to simply end the conflict on those terms.

Resolutions

The United Nations proposed a cease-fire on all sides. On October 22, the UN Security Council adopted Resolution 338.

U.S. secretary of state Henry Kissinger crafted a deal for peace between Israel and Egypt. On November 12, 1973, journalists and United Nations soldiers gathered to witness the signing of the Kissinger Agreement.

It called for everyone involved in the war to stop fighting immediately. Israel chose to acknowledge the cease-fire. It stopped all attacks. This was the only thing that saved Egypt's Third Army from total destruction. It had attempted to break free from the south, but Sharon had simply moved his forces farther south of the Suez. By October 24, Israel held more than 1,000 square miles (2,590 sq km) of Egypt.

On October 26, Egypt finally stopped fighting. The Yom Kippur War was officially over.

Many Israelis did not want this cease-fire. Egypt's Third Army was trapped on the Sinai east of the Suez Canal, and the Israeli army could have crushed it. But Kissinger reasoned that Egypt would be more willing to make peace if it could keep some of its initial gains. The cease-fire was shaky. The troop lines were intertwined. Most observers feared that fighting would resume shortly. U.S. forces were put on red alert the next day, allegedly because Soviet ships were unloading nuclear warheads at Alexandria, Egypt. Nevertheless, the cease-fire held.

Syria refused to abide by the initial cease-fire, however, and continued to launch attacks on Israel, despite being badly outmatched and having Damascus in danger.

Discussions

Once the fighting stopped, the new problem became one of territory. Egypt and Syria had tried to reclaim land that Israel had taken from them in the Six-Day War. Instead, the two nations had now lost additional territory. Israel had taken

Henry Kissinger: United States Secretary of State (1973–1977)

Henry Alfred Kissinger was born in Fuerth, Germany, on May 27, 1923. His family moved to New York City in 1938. Kissinger became a naturalized United States citizen in 1943. He received his degree from Harvard in 1950, after spending several years in the army as a German interpreter. Later, he earned a doctoral degree. In 1968, President Richard Nixon appointed Kissinger national security adviser. Kissinger established détente (truce among equals) with the Soviet Union and negotiated several key arms treaties. He and Le Duc Tho of Vietnam received the Nobel Peace Prize in 1973 for the Vietnam peace accords. Tho refused to accept the award, however, because Kissinger had overseen several illegal bombing campaigns in Laos and Cambodia. In 1973, Nixon appointed Kissinger as U.S. secretary of state, and President Ford renewed his appointment.

more than 150 square miles (388 sq km) of Syrian land and was now camped on the western bank of the Suez Canal. On the other hand, Egypt still held two locations on the eastern bank of the canal, in what had been Israeli territory. All three nations had prisoners of war.

The United States headed talks between the nations. The Soviet Union helped push the peace process. It proposed a Middle East peace conference in Geneva in late December. Unfortunately, Syria refused to attend because Israel had not yet evacuated what had been Syrian lands. Syria's resistance made Egypt hesitate as well. After this, Kissinger, who had been handling most of the negotiations, concentrated on bilateral agreements. He focused on dealing with Israel and just one of the other nations, rather than trying to get all three to agree at once. This became known as shuttle diplomacy because Kissinger kept shuttling back and forth between the various nations and their leaders.

Agreement

In January 1974, Israel finally signed the First Sinai Disengagement Agreement. This called for its troops to

Israeli soldiers mourn the loss of their fallen comrades in 1974. The bodies of the Israeli soldiers were returned to Israel for suitable burial. Several rows of coffins containing the dead are honored by fellow soldiers.

withdraw back across the Suez. The Second Disengagement Agreement, signed in September 1975, had Israel withdraw from the Sinai passes as well. This also returned a portion of the Suez's western bank to Egypt. The agreements also called for a buffer zone between the two nations. The zones would be patrolled by UN forces. Israel was not happy with these concessions—it felt it had won the war. The United States, however, pressured Israel to agree. On March 5, 1974, Israeli forces withdrew from the canal's western bank, and Egypt assumed control.

Syria and Israel continued to attack one another, though on a smaller scale, for several months after the official cease-fire. The two nations finally signed a disengagement agreement on May 31, 1974. Now UN forces patrolled the Golan to maintain the peace. Israel was forced to surrender the territory it had gained during the Yom Kippur War, and it also gave up some of the land it had taken in the 1967 war.

Between November 15 and November 22, 1973, all sides exchanged prisoners of war. Egypt and Israel also returned POWs they had held since the War of Attrition. Although Israel had managed to drive back the Arab forces, the price had been high. More than 2,500 soldiers were killed, and more than 150 planes had been destroyed.

CHAPTER 6

LASTING IMPRESSIONS

SALES LIMITED
PER CUSTOMER
TO
10 GALLONS·GASOLINE
35 GALLONS·DIESEL

WE REGRET ANY
INCONVENIENCE

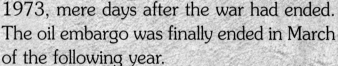

Planning a war usually takes longer than the war itself. But the results of a war can last for years, decades, and even centuries. In the Middle East, where the countries are constantly struggling against one another, the aftermath of a war can be as important as the battles themselves.

The Arab nations were not happy with the outcome of the Yom Kippur War. In protest, they began an oil embargo against those nations that had supported Israel. This started in October 1973, mere days after the war had ended. The oil embargo was finally ended in March of the following year.

Israel's enemies had learned an important lesson that October. They discovered that the Jewish homeland had an impressive military, even when surprised and outnumbered. After the Yom Kippur War, the Arab nations stopped launching all-out wars against Israel. They continued to harass the nation with raids and small attacks, but they turned most of their attention to diplomatic warfare instead. These nations began to pressure others to break off ties with Israel, in hopes of isolating the nation.

In 1975, the Arab nations, along with the Soviets and several third world powers, convinced the United Nations

A sign at an American gas station requests its customers to buy only small amounts of gasoline. Gasoline was scarce during the 1973 embargo, and prices soared. Drivers waited in long lines for hours to refill their tanks.

The Syrian village Hadar was devastated by the Israeli counterattack. Syrian villagers look toward a United Nations post on the border between Syria and Israel. Angered by the outcome of the Yom Kippur War, Syrians demanded the return of the Golan Heights, but were refused.

that Zionism was in fact racist (placing the welfare of one group over all others on the basis of heritage alone). They hoped that this would convince others that the Jews had no right to a land of their own. The UN finally revoked Resolution 3379 in 1991.

Many of the Arab nations had lost a great deal, both in terms of manpower (more than 8,500 Arab soldiers were killed) and money. This increased their dependence on the Soviet Union. It also caused shifts within several Arab governments. King Faisal of Saudi Arabia was assassinated in 1975 and replaced by his half-brother, Khalid. Fundamentalists within Syria tried to overthrow the Baath Party from 1976 to 1982. Assad did crush the rebellion but only after leveling part of the city of Hama and leaving thousands dead or wounded. This turmoil allowed the Soviet Union to gain even more influence over these nations, by offering support and aid during these situations.

Not every nation turned away from the West, however. Egypt and Syria had had little contact with the United States before the war. During the peace process, however, they reopened diplomatic relations, which continued afterward. This renewed contact led the way to Sadat's surprising decision to make peace with Israel and to agree to the Camp David Accords.

Israel also suffered problems after the war. Approximately 6,000 soldiers were killed or wounded during the war. Israel spent as much money on the war as it normally made in one year. Israeli leaders knew that they could not afford many more battles like this. As a result, Israel became more dependent on the United States for aid. The nation was also divided on what to do about the territories gained in 1967. Some felt it should keep the land and fortify it against attack, while others thought it should be returned to prevent further conflict. Golda Meir resigned her post as prime minister after the war, and Moshe Dayan left as well. Many felt that Israeli intelligence had failed in its job by not anticipating the attack. Israel became less confident and more cautious.

In 1988, Jordan formally renounced any claim to the West Bank. It had recognized the Palestine Liberation Organization (PLO) as the official representative of Palestine in 1974 and acknowledged that the West Bank was Palestinian territory. This created new problems for Israel. Palestinians were already accusing the Israelis of stealing their homeland. Now a neighboring nation had recognized an area of Israel as belonging to that group.

The Middle East continues to be an area filled with problems and conflicts. Fighting has continued to this day. Some fighting has been on a small scale. Other, larger battles, have involved outside nations. The Yom Kippur War was the last time the Arab nations tried attacking Israel directly.

GLOSSARY

Aman   The Israeli intelligence agency.

Baath   A fundamentalist party of Arab nationalists. Baath groups have appeared in several Middle East nations, including Egypt and Syria.

countermeasures   In military terms, devices and techniques used to avoid being targeted or hit by missiles and other weapons.

embargo   When one nation deliberately refuses to ship or receive products from another nation. The idea is to attack the other nation economically by limiting its trade and hurting profits.

kibbutz   A communal farming village, where everyone works equally and shares equally.

Knesset   Israel's parliament, equivalent to the United States Congress.

missile array   A collection of missiles, either in a single launch structure or simply linked together, that can be aimed and fired as a unit.

Ramadan   A major Islamic holiday.

Rosh Hashanah   The Jewish New Year.

Yom Kippur   The Jewish day of atonement, a major holiday.

Organizations

The Abraham Fund Initiatives
477 Madison Avenue, Fourth Floor
New York, NY 10022
(800) 301-FUND (3863)
e-mail: info@abrahamfund.org
Web site: http://www.abrahamfund.org

The Arab Organization for Human Rights (AOHR)
91 Al-Marghany Street
Heliopolis, Cairo, Egypt
e-mail: aohr@link.com.eg
Web site: http://www.aohr.org

Zionist Organization of America
4 East 34th Street
New York, NY 10016
(212) 481-1500
e-mail: info@zoa.org
Web site: http://www.zoa.org

Web Sites

Due to the changing nature of Internet links, the Rosen Publishing Group, Inc., has developed an online list of Web sites related to the subject of this book. This site is updated regularly. Please use this link to access the list:

http://www.rosenlinks.com/wcme/yokw

Altman, Linda Jacobs, ed. *The Creation of Israel* (World History). Chicago: Lucent, 1998.

Harris, Nathaniel, and Hopkins Harris. *Israel and the Arab Nations in Conflict* (New Perspectives). New York: Raintree/Steck Vaughn, 1999.

Hitzeroth, Deborah. *Golda Meir* (Importance of). Chicago: Lucent, 1997.

McAleavy, Tony. *The Arab-Israeli Conflict*. New York: SIGS Books & Multimedia, 1998.

Minnis, Ivan.*The Arab-Israeli Conflict* (Troubled World Series). New York: Raintree/Steck Vaughn, 2003.

Silverman, Maida. *Israel: The Founding of a Modern Nation*. New York: Dial, 1998.

BIBLIOGRAPHY

Ghali, Mazen Abu. "Hafez Al-Assad Profile." Retrieved April
        21, 2003 (http://www.la.utexas.edu/chenry/mena/
        roles/oil/1998/0075.html).

"Golda Meir." Women's International Center. Retrieved April
        20, 2003 (http://www.wic.org/bio/gmeir.htm).

Jabri, Sami (and Syrian Internet). "President Hafez Al-Assad
        in Profile." Assad.org. Retrieved April 21, 2003
        (http://assad.org/profile.htm).

Kahalani, Avigdor. *The Heights of Courage: A Tank
        Leader's War on the Golan.* New York: Praeger, 1992.

"King Hussein I." Who2.com. Retrieved April 17, 2003
        (http://www.who2.com/kinghusseini.html).

"The 1973 Yom Kippur War." Anti-Defamation League.
        Retrieved March 21, 2003 (http://www.adl.org/
        israel/record/yomkippur.asp).

Reich, Bernard, ed. *An Historical Encyclopedia of the
        Arab-Israeli Conflict.* New York: Greenwood, 1996.

Rich, Tracey R. "Yom Kippur." Judaism 101. Retrieved
        March 12, 2003 (http://www.jewfaq.org/holiday4.htm).

Trautman, Robin. "The Yom Kippur War." Retrieved
        February 21, 2003 (http://campus.northpark.edu/
        history/webchron/middleeast/yomkippurwar.html).

"Yom Kippur War." Retrieved February 18, 2003 (http://
        www.fas.org/man/dod-101/ops/yom_kippur.htm).

INDEX

About the Author

Aaron Rosenberg is a writer and the owner of a gaming company (http://www.clockworksgames.com). He lives in New York.

Photo Credits

Cover, pp. 1, 40–41 © Chauvel Genevieve/Corbis; p. 3 © Wheeler Nik/Corbis; pp. 4–5, 10, 14, 52 © David Rubinger/Corbis; pp. 6–7 © Corbis; pp. 12, 16, 54–55 © Bettmann/Corbis; pp. 18–19, 20, 26, 30, 32–33, 35, 36, 49 © Hulton/Archive/Getty Images; p. 23 © Wally McNamee/Corbis; p. 25 © Peter Turnley/Corbis; p. 43 © Hulton-Deutsch/Corbis; pp. 46–47 © Dejean Alian/Corbis; p. 56 © Reuters New Media Inc.

Designer: Nelson Sá; **Editor:** Mark Beyer;
Photo Researcher: Nelson Sá.